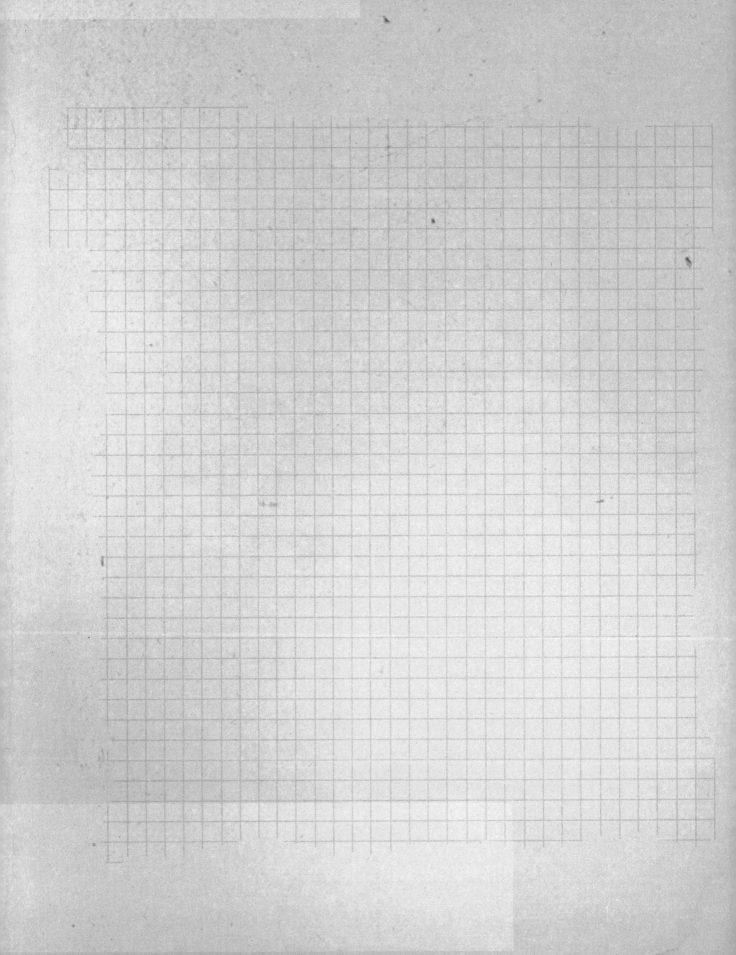

HOW TO DESIGN THE WORLD'S BEST BIKE

IN 10 SIMPLE STEPS

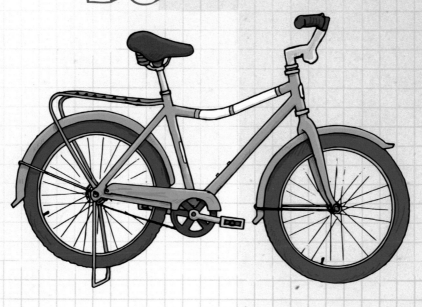

PAUL MASON

WAYLAND
www.waylandbooks.co.uk

First published in Great Britain in 2016 by
Hodder and Stoughton Limited

Copyright © Wayland, 2016

Editor: Nicola Edwards
Design: Kevin Knight

Artwork by Tim Hutchinson

ISBN: 978 0 7502 9996 1

10 9 8 7 6 5 4 3 2 1

Wayland, an imprint of
Hachette Children's Group
Part of Hodder and Stoughton
Carmelite House
50 Victoria Embankment
London EC4Y 0DZ

An Hachette UK Company
www.hachette.co.uk
www.hachettechildrens.co.uk

Printed and bound in China

Picture acknowledgements:
All images courtesy of Shutterstock.

CONTENTS

DESIGNING THE WORLD'S BEST BIKE

Bikes are brilliant. Riding a bike is a fast way to get around, it keeps you fit, makes you live longer – it could even make you more brainy! Imagine being asked to design a bike yourself.

This is not just any old bike you are going to design. This bike is going to help kids in Africa get an education, by making it easier for them to get to school.

Research Note

In many parts of Africa, children live a long distance from the nearest school. To get there, they have to walk.

To make the journey easier, charities have started reconditioning old bicycles. Then they give the bikes to poor families. The children can ride to school in far less time than it takes to walk.

The bicycles can also be used as family transport, for taking goods to market, or even for collecting water.

Any bike is better than no bike – but this young man would find it easier to pedal something slightly smaller.

WORK IT OUT!

If the average walking speed is 5kph, how long does it take to walk 8km to school? Work it out like this:

• In 60 minutes, you can walk 5km.

• Divide 60 by 5 to get how many minutes it takes to walk 1km.

• Multiply the answer by 8

Next, work out how long it would take you to cycle, at an average speed of 12kph.

Check your answers on page 31.

A good bike can take you to the top of a tall mountain.

RESEARCHING THE DESIGN

This will be a brand-new bike. Its owners will be people with little money. The bike has to be inexpensive and long-lasting.

The first step in designing the bike is to find out more about where and how it will be used. (Pages 6–7 will help with this.) Next do some research into possible designs. There are lots of places to get information about bicycle designs:

1) Your own experience

What kind of bike do you and your friends ride? Would any of your bikes be a good design?

2) Books and the Internet

There are lots of books and websites about different types of bike. Some of the subjects you could find out about are:
- long-distance cycling
- touring bicycles
- commuter bicycles
- off-road bicycles

3) Bike shops

People who work in bike shops usually know a LOT about bikes. If you go in at a quiet time and describe what the bike is going to be used for, they might give you some advice.

Bikes are a great way to get around in crowded cities. They take up much less space than cars, and cause no air pollution.

THE IDEAL BIKE

A successful design will have to do exactly what the African children using it need. Below is an interview with a girl called Pamela. There are millions of kids like Pamela in Africa. The interview provides some ideas for the kind of bike they need.

Walking to school (and then home again) takes some kids in Africa hours.

FACT FILE
NAME: Pamela Chikanda
AGE: 13
COUNTRY: Zambia

Where do you live?
In a small village in Zambia. I live with my mum and dad, and my younger brother.

A small village will not have a bike shop. So the bike needs to be tough, and easy to repair if anything does go wrong with it.

How far is your journey to school?
School is 8km away. I walk: there is no bus, but my parents could not afford bus fares anyway.

How does your day begin?
I get up at 05.00 to get to school by 07.00. I'm often late, and miss the first part of lessons. We finish at 12.00.

Pamela's bike will need to cost as little as possible.

What are the roads like?
Most of the way it is a dirt road. In the dry the road is hard, bumpy and dusty. If it rains, the road quickly gets muddy. There are a few hills, but none of them are very steep or long.

The bike has to work on bumpy roads. It should also be rideable in both dusty and wet/muddy conditions.

What effect does the long journey have on you?
The journey is so hard that I only go to school 3 days a week. Sometimes I find it hard to concentrate, or just fall asleep in lessons.

If you had a bicycle, could your family use it?
Yes: my father could use it to carry his crops. And I could give my little brother lifts!

The bike has to be able to carry heavy loads. It needs to fit lots of different-sized riders (ranging from Pamela to her dad).

This bike is being used as a combined pushchair and wheelbarrow.

WORK IT OUT!

Use the interview to make a shortlist of things the bike has to do. For example, one of them could be, 'must be tough'.

Later, when you test each part of the design, this shortlist (or 'design brief') will help you make decisions. For example, thin tyres would not be best for bumpy roads. Wide tyres would absorb the bumps much better.

Check your thinking against the design brief on pages 8 and 31.

MAKE A DREAM DESIGN

You have read the interview with Pamela (pages 6 and 7). You have researched all sorts of different bikes designs. It is time to pick up a pencil and start sketching a dream design. (It might be a good idea to pick up an eraser too. No design is ever perfect first time...)

Suspension forks and seat post
Absorb bumps on rough roads
Fork can be locked out when cycling uphill

AFRICA BIKE DESIGN BRIEF
The bike has to be:
- Tough
- Reliable
- Cheap
- Comfortable on bumpy roads
- Easy to repair
- Good in dusty and wet/muddy conditions
- Able to carry loads
- Suitable for riders of different sizes

8 gears on the back wheel, 3 gears on the cranks
3 x 8 = 24 gears to choose from
Easy to pedal uphill, fast going downhill

A bike and trailer together means the trailer can be unhitched when the bike is not carrying loads. The bike can be lighter: it does not need to be as strongly built if it is not going to be weighed down with stuff.

Trailer for carrying goods
Attaches to frame
Can be unhitched when not needed

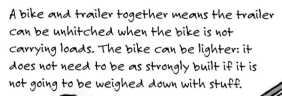

Aluminium frame
Light frame to make the bike faster

Disc brakes
Total stopping power in wet and dry conditions

FROM DREAM DESIGN TO REAL BIKE?

Of course, this sketch is a dream design. Before building the bike in the real world, you need to check every part of the design. This makes sure that when it is built, the bike will match the design brief.

So, the next steps in designing the bike are to look in more detail at everything – to see whether the dream can be turned into a real-life ride.

PICK THE FRAME MATERIAL

The original design showed a bike with a frame made out of aluminium. Most modern bikes have aluminium (often called 'alloy') frames. But is alloy the best material for the bike for Africa?

DREAM DESIGN

ALLOY V. STEEL

Alloy is usually chosen because it is lighter than steel, the other main metal used for bicycle frames. But this is not the whole story. Some of the other differences between the two could be important for this design:

Research Note

Weight and strength: Alloy is lighter than steel, but steel is stronger. This means an alloy bike frame has to have bigger and thicker tubes than a steel one.

Toughness: Steel is tougher than alloy. Alloy behaves a bit like glass: if you bend it, it cracks. Steel can be scratched, dented and bent without breaking.

Comfort: Steel is more flexible than alloy. This means that as a bike goes over bumps, the frame can absorb a little bit of the shock. On an alloy bike, the shock goes straight to the rider's hands and bottom.

Repairability: If steel breaks it can be repaired with basic welding equipment. Repairing alloy is more difficult and can be impossible.

Environment: Making alloy uses more energy than making steel, and more metal is needed for an alloy frame.

BMX bikes – which have to be tough! – are usually made out of steel.

Race bikes, which need to be light rather than tough, are often made of aluminium.

WORK IT OUT!

Use the information from the research note, plus the design brief from page 7, to decide between alloy and steel. You could set out the pluses and minuses as in the table on the right.

See which metal does best in the most categories of the design brief. This would be the best one to use.

Check your ideas on page 31.

Design brief:	Alloy?	Steel?
Tough		
Comfortable on bumpy roads		
Reliable	Not relevant	
Cheap		Slightly less expensive
Easy to repair		
Good in dry and wet conditions	Not relevant	
Able to carry loads	Yes	Yes
Suitable for riders of different size	Not relevant	

THE FINAL DESIGN

After comparing the two metals, it seems that the bike for Africa's frame should be steel. It is tough, comfortable and easy to repair, which are important parts of the design brief. Steel's characteristics – such as being flexible – might also have an effect on other parts of the design.

REVISED DESIGN

CONSIDER ROUGH GROUND AND COMFORT

The design brief says the bike should be comfortable on rough ground. The original design for the bike has shock-absorbing forks and a shock-absorbing seat post. These would absorb bumps as the bike goes over rough ground. But do the shock absorbers fit with other parts of the design brief?

DREAM DESIGN

Research Note

Suspension on bicycles has been around since at least the 1890s. Modern suspension uses metal springs (or similar devices) to absorb shocks.

Suspension adds weight and cost, but it is common on off-road bikes.

To work properly, modern suspension has to be kept free of dirt and water. Unless cleaned and serviced regularly it is likely to fail.

SUSPENSION OR NOT?

After checking the design brief against the RESEARCH NOTE, it seems that the shock-absorbing forks and seat post might have to be removed from the design:

Design brief:	Suspension
Tough	No
Comfortable on bumpy roads	Yes
Reliable	No, unless serviced
Cheap	No
Easy to repair	No
Good in dry and wet conditions	Wet/muddy/dusty conditions not ideal

There are too many 'no' answers!

It is still important that the bike is as comfortable to ride as possible, though. As designer, it is your job to work out how to achieve this.

Modern bike suspension is complicated and has to be looked after carefully.

WORK IT OUT!

The Africa bike needs to be as comfortable as possible. How can you achieve this?

The parts of the rider's body that touch the bike are called the 'contact points'. Do some research to find out about ways of making the contact points more comfortable.

Part of your research should be to ride as many different bikes as possible. Which are most comfortable, and what is it that makes them comfortable? (Hint: try a bike where you sit quite upright, then one where you are stretched out with a lot of weight on your hands. Which is the most comfortable riding position?)

Below are a few photographic clues too. Check what you have found out on page 31.

THE FINAL DESIGN

The design has now changed quite a lot. The original shock-absorbing features have gone. They have been replaced by a simpler, cheaper, more reliable design. The bike has higher, wider handlebars so that less of Pamela's weight will be on her hands. They can be tilted, lowered or raised to suit different riders. And the wide, slightly padded seat will be more comfortable.

REVISED DESIGN

FINALISE THE FRAME

The next job is to make final adjustments to the frame design. Ever since the 1800s, almost every bicycle frame has been the same shape. The design is two near-triangles, which share a side (the seat tube). Small changes to this basic design can have a BIG effect on the final bike.

Research Note

Some of the most important measurements in a bike frame, and how they affect the design:

Seat tube

A long seat tube means the saddle will not go low enough for small riders.

A very short seat tube means the saddle will not go high enough for tall riders.

Top-tube drop

The difference between how far above the ground the top tube is at one end from the other. The top tube is almost always higher at the front of a bike.

Wheelbase

The distance between the middles of the front and back wheels. The bike's wheelbase affects its handling: longer = slower turning, shorter = faster turning.

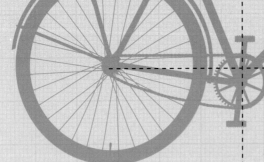

Chain- and seat-stay length

These decide how far behind the rider the rear wheel will be.

Standover height

The distance above the ground of a bike's top tube, at the place where a cyclist would stand with their feet on the ground. If your legs are shorter than the standover height, it makes it impossible to stop and put both feet on the ground.

WORK IT OUT!

The design brief asks for the bike to suit as many different-sized riders as possible.

At the moment, this is causing problems. Pamela has 69cm legs, but her dad has 86cm legs. They need a frame with a long seat tube, so the saddle can go high enough for dad's long legs. But the bike also needs a low standover height for Pamela.

Look at as many different bike designs as you can, in this book and on the Internet, to see if you can find a solution. There are at least three.

You can check your ideas on page 31.

DESIGN CHANGES

It would be a good idea to make some changes to the design of the frame. Based on the work on these pages, there are several changes that would be a good idea:

Some small details of the frame might still need to change. They could be affected by the wheel size (page 16) and tyres (page 18). But the frame design is now almost finished.

Longer chainstays + bigger fork offset = longer wheelbase for more predictable turns (especially important when carrying a load!)

Shorter standover height

Same top-tube drop

Curved top tube

REVISED DESIGN

DECIDE THE WHEEL SIZE

There are three main wheel sizes for bikes: 26er, 27.5er and 29er. The measurements come from the wheel's diameter. Each size has different strengths and weaknesses. In the original design, the wheel size isn't actually clear. So the next design job is to decide which wheel size will be best for the Africa bike.

The basic rule is that big wheels roll over obstacles easily, but are heavy and slow to get up to speed. Small wheels are not as smooth, but turn and accelerate better.

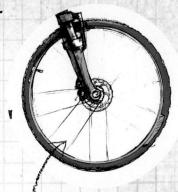

Wheels – how big is best?

DREAM DESIGN

Research Note

26er wheels

Used on: beach cruisers, mountain bikes

Characteristics: strength, fast acceleration, quick turns, suitable for riders of all sizes

Availability/cost of spares and tyres: cheap; widely available

29er wheels

Used on: modern mountain bikes, road bikes

Characteristics: heavy, roll over bumps well, slow to accelerate, only suitable for riders over 175cm tall

Availability/cost of spares and tyres: higher price than 26er; good in wealthy countries

27.5er wheels

Used on: modern mountain bikes, some touring bikes

Characteristics: midway between 26er and 29er; not suitable for very short riders

Availability of spares and tyres: higher price than 26er; can be hard to find

Cruiser

Race bike

Mountain bike

WORK IT OUT!

Based on the research note, score each wheel size according to which gets the most points in each category of the design brief (3 is best, 1 is worst):

You can check your ideas on page 31.

Design brief:	26er	29er	27.5er
Tough	3	1	2
Comfortable on bumpy roads			
Reliable			
Cheap			
Easy to repair			
Good in dry and wet conditions			
Able to carry loads			
Suitable for riders of different size			
Total			

THE FINAL DESIGN

The final design is for a bike with 26er wheels. This wheel size has three knockout advantages that the other sizes cannot match:

1) It is suitable for riders of all sizes – even as different as Pamela and her dad.

2) It is the strongest wheel size – so it is best for carrying loads and least likely to need repair.

3) Spares and tyres are available in Africa – if something does go wrong, repairs should be easy.

REVISED DESIGN

CHOOSE THE TYRES

The tyres you put on a bike make a BIG difference to the way it rides. The original design shows skinny tyres, like you see on bikes in the Tour de France. These look fast – but now it's time to work out whether they are the best tyres for the Africa bike.

DREAM DESIGN

BACK TO THE DESIGN BRIEF

When choosing the best tyre, there are four key parts of the design brief to remember:
• The tyre has to be tough
• It has to be comfortable on bumpy roads
• Good in dusty and wet/muddy conditions
• Able to carry loads

TOUGH AND COMFORTABLE

On a bike, the tyres act as shock absorbers, making the ride more comfortable. When the bike hits a bump, the tyre squishes down a bit. This stops the whole bump being transmitted to the rider.

Research Note

Zambia has two main seasons: the wet season (Nov–April) and the dry season (May–Oct).

The wettest months are December, January, February and March. At this time of year it rains most days, usually as a result of thunderstorms in the afternoon.

WORK IT OUT!

Will a big or small tyre be best at absorbing shocks? Look at these two diagrams:

Grab a ruler, and check what would happen to each tyre if it hit a rock and squashed down by 2cm. Check your thinking on page 31.

DRY, WET, MUDDY – EVERYTHING!

There is one more decision to make. What kind of tread should the tyre have? Should it have knobbly tyres like a mountain bike? Or smoother tyres like a beach cruiser?

• Knobbly tyres have good grip. This is especially useful uphill. The knobs do sometimes get clogged with mud, though. Some of this usually ends up on the rider's face, or back. Knobbly tyres do not work well with mudguards.

• Smooth tyres lose grip in mud. They work well with mudguards, though, so are good for keeping the rider dry.

WORK IT OUT!

Look at the RESEARCH NOTES and work out what the road will be like when Pamela is going to and from school. (Remember, her school day starts at 07.00 and finishes at 12.00, and it will be a 40-minute journey.)

Does this affect your decision about what kind of tyre the bike should have? Check your ideas on page 31.

THE FINAL DESIGN

In response to the times of day the bike will be used, the final design is for fat, but not knobbly, tyres. The basic design of the bike – the frame, wheels and tyres – is now complete: There are just a few crucial details (the gears and brakes) to complete!

REVISED DESIGN

PICK THE GEARING

The original design showed a bike with derailleur gears. On a bike like this, the rider can choose between up to 33 different gears. They can climb up the steepest hills and pedal down the other side at high speed.

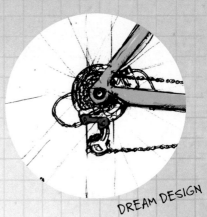

DREAM DESIGN

CHECKING THE DESIGN BRIEF

Good designers are constantly checking that their design fits the original list of requirements. Do derailleur gears fit the list of requirements from page 5? This bike has to be:

tough, reliable, cheap, comfortable on bumpy roads, easy to repair, good in dusty and wet/muddy conditions, able to carry loads, and suitable for riders of different sizes

Climbing steep hills and racing down the other side is not mentioned – so are derailleur gears the best choice?

Research Note

There are three main types of bicycle gear:

1 Derailleur gears

These are light and relatively inexpensive.

The choice of gears makes cycling up and down steep, long hills easier.

They are easily damaged, and not good in muddy conditions.

2 Hub gears

Hub gears are heavy and can be expensive.

They provide between 2 and 14 gears.

The gears are hidden inside the wheel, so they are tough. Repairs are tricky.

3 Single speed

This is light and cheap.

A single-speed bike has just one gear: OK on flat ground or small hills, but not steep hills.

Single speed gears rarely break.

Derailleur

Hub

Single Speed

WORK IT OUT!

Decide which type of gear will be best for the Africa bike.

Give each type a score of between 1 and 3 (3 is best, 1 is worst). Base your scoring on the research note, as in the table on the right.

Use the scores to help you decide which gear will be best for Pamela's bike. Check your thinking on page 31.

Design brief:	Derailleur	Hub	Single speed
Tough	1		
Comfortable on bumpy roads	not applicable		
Reliable			
Cheap			
Easy to repair			
Good in dry and wet conditions		2.5	2.5
Able to carry loads	3	2	1
Suitable for riders of different size	not applicable		
Total			

THE FINAL DESIGN

The scoring will show that no design is perfect. None of the choices get top score in every category. One type of gear is the clear winner. It is not the original derailleur design – it is a single speed.

REVISED DESIGN

BRAKES

The original design for the Africa bike shows disc brakes. Disc brakes are powerful. They are good at stopping bikes travelling at high speed. They work well in the wet. So, could there be any reason to change this design decision?

DREAM DESIGN

DISC-BRAKE DECISION

There are lots of good things about disc brakes, but they are not perfect. They are expensive and heavy. If they go wrong or break, the cost of replacement or repair is high. Disc brakes are complicated, too, so working on them is a specialist job.

Even so, disc brakes might still be needed if the bike will be going fast. Then it would need to have powerful brakes for safety.

Research Note

Coaster brakes are hidden inside a bike's back wheel. The rider slows down by pedalling backwards.

A back-wheel coaster brake is about 65% as powerful as having brakes on both wheels. The advantage of coaster brakes is that they are more reliable and need less maintenance than other brakes.

Research Note

Bicycle gears are measured in a unit called 'metres of development'. This describes how far the bicycle will travel with every complete turn of the pedals. A gear with a 3-metre development, for example, travels 3m every time the pedals turn.

Coaster brake

WORK IT OUT!

How fast will Pamela be able to pedal the Africa bike? Here are the two pieces of information needed for working it out:

1) The bike chain will go around a 40-tooth cog at the front, and a 20-tooth cog at the back. This creates a gear with 4.2m of development (see the research note).

2) The maximum number of times most people can comfortably turn the pedals in a minute is 70.

Check your answers on page 31.

ALTERNATIVE BRAKES

Here are some bikes, their maximum speeds, and the types of brake they use. Comparing them to the Africa bike's top speed (from the WORK IT OUT! panel) might help decide what kind of brakes the bike should have:

Bike:	Top speed:	Type of brakes:
Downhill mountain bike	65kph	Disc brakes
Road race bike	110kph	Rim brakes
City bike	30kph	Rim or coaster brake
Cruiser	15kph	Coaster brake

A back-wheel coaster brake is about 65% as powerful as having brakes on both wheels. The advantage of coaster brakes is that they are more reliable and need less maintenance than other brakes.

Rim brake

THE FINAL DESIGN

The final design is for a bike with a coaster brake. This type of brake is not affected by wet or mud. It will probably last for years without needing attention. If something does eventually go wrong, coaster brakes are easy to work on.

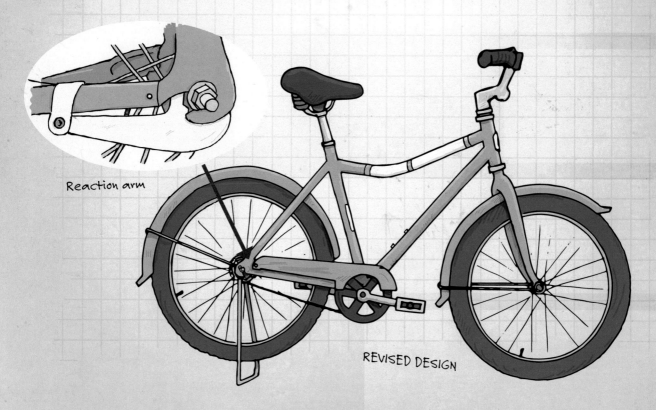

Reaction arm

REVISED DESIGN

LOAD LUGGING

It is important that the Africa bike can be used to transport loads. In her interview, Pamela said her dad would use the bike to take his crops to market. She also plans to use it for giving her little brother lifts.

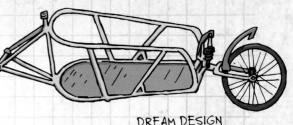

DREAM DESIGN

The original design was for a bike with a detachable trailer. There are two problems with the trailer, though:
1) It would add about 20% to the overall cost
2) Although the trailer would be good for transporting crops, it would not be as good at transporting little brothers!

WORK IT OUT!

Find an alternative to the trailer. Use the Internet to research other ways of carrying luggage or a passenger on a bike. Image searches using these terms will give you some ideas:

bicycle + load carrying (this gives some crazy results!)

pannier rack

bicycle + passenger

Always use a variety of search engines, not only Google. This gives a variety of results.

Which method looks best? Check your thinking on page 31.

This rear rack has been screwed to holes in the frame.

Rear racks are not only for luggage.

THE FINAL DESIGN

The Africa bike will have a rack for carrying loads and passengers. The strongest place to put the rack is on the back of the bike. There are two ways to attach a rear rack. You can bolt it to the frame, or it can be welded into place.

Welding the rack to the frame is the strongest way to attach it, so this would be the best choice. To make loading easier, the bike will also need a strong, well-balanced stand.

WORK IT OUT!

How wide should the rack be?

It needs to be wide enough to sit on or carry loads, but not SO wide that it adds unnecessary weight.

Experiment with your friends to find the ideal width. Try sitting on the edge of a table, as close to the edge as you can without slipping off. Measure how far in from the edge you are sitting. Imagine being a passenger on the back of a bike with that much space to sit. Is it enough?

REVISED DESIGN

DECIDE COLOURS AND GRAPHICS

The Africa bike's design is almost complete. There is really just one thing still to decide: the colour and graphics. Painting the bike is important, as it will stop the steel frame from getting rusty. Plus, like any designer, you want the design to look as good as possible!

PAINT TECHNIQUE

There are two main ways to paint a bike frame. One is spray painting, the other is powder coating. Powder coating will be best for the Africa bike. It is tough, inexpensive and less environmentally harmful than spray painting.

The only problem with powder coating is that it is tricky to powder coat the frame with more than one colour. This means each Africa bike will be one colour.

WORK IT OUT!

The Africa bike will be available in two colours. Use the research note to help you decide on the best ones.

Take photocopies or scan the blank bike frame. Colour them in to check on the colours and shades you think look best.

WORK IT OUT!

First, decide on a typeface for your graphics. The maximum height of the letters has to be 30mm, or the stickers will not fit on the frame. Here are two to get you started.

Arial Bold:

Africa Bike AFRICA BIKE AFRICA BIKE

Akzidenz Bold Condensed:

Africa Bike AFRICA BIKE AFRICA BIKE

You can find inspiration for other possible fonts, such as Phosphate and Chilada, on the Internet.

Next, use a computer to pick colours. Make a background colour the same as you have picked for the bike frame. Change the typeface colour until you have found the one that works best.

Research Note

Colours have different meanings depending on where you live. In parts of Africa, these colours are said to have special meaning:

RED: death and mourning in South Africa; chiefs and ceremonies in western Africa

YELLOW: wealth and high rank

BLUE: happiness and good luck

GREEN: in South Africa, nature; in northern Africa, dishonesty

BLACK: age and wisdom

GRAPHICS

Adding graphic stickers to the frame will advertise the bike to other people. They will know where to get a cheap, strong, reliable bike. The graphics will need to be easy to read and look good against the main colour of the bike.

Yellow is a popular colour at this wedding in Nigeria!

THE BEST EVER BIKE?

Every part of the bike has now been checked. You have looked at the frame, wheels, tyres, gears, brakes and other parts to make sure they will do their jobs as well as possible. The design is complete.

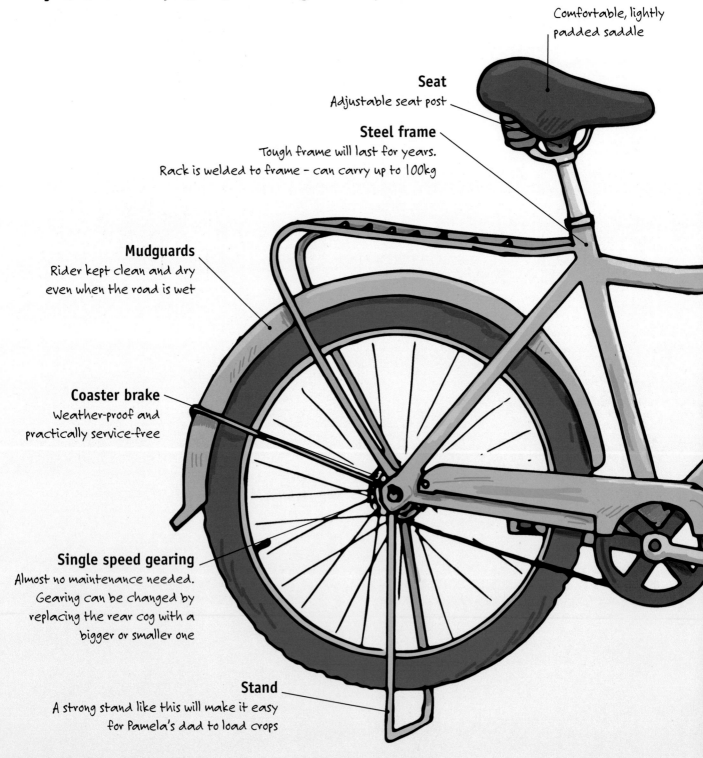

Comfortable, lightly padded saddle

Seat
Adjustable seat post

Steel frame
Tough frame will last for years.
Rack is welded to frame – can carry up to 100kg

Mudguards
Rider kept clean and dry even when the road is wet

Coaster brake
Weather-proof and practically service-free

Single speed gearing
Almost no maintenance needed. Gearing can be changed by replacing the rear cog with a bigger or smaller one

Stand
A strong stand like this will make it easy for Pamela's dad to load crops

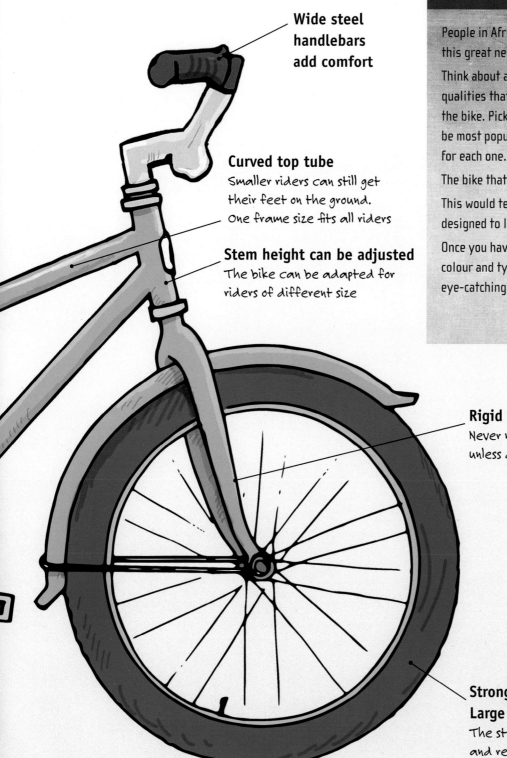

Wide steel handlebars add comfort

Curved top tube
Smaller riders can still get their feet on the ground. One frame size fits all riders

Stem height can be adjusted
The bike can be adapted for riders of different size

Rigid forks
Never need attention unless damaged

Strong 26er wheels
Large tyres
The strongest, most comfortable and reliable choice

WORK IT OUT!

People in Africa need to know about this great new bike design!

Think about all the features and qualities that have been designed into the bike. Pick the three you think will be most popular, and make a slogan for each one. For example:

The bike that lasts a lifetime!

This would tell people that the bike is designed to last a long, long time.

Once you have three slogans, use colour and typefaces to design an eye-catching poster.

OTHER TOP BIKES

The Africa bike is probably the best design in the world. The best, that is, for getting African kids like Pamela to school. There are lots of other bike designs that are just as good at the job they were designed for. Here are a few of them:

BMX BIKE
COMPANY: DK Bicycles Pro model
RELEASED: 2015
MATERIAL: Aluminium
USED FOR: BMX
This bike must be good: it's the model used by Jamie Bestwick to win his record-smashing NINTH X-Games vert BMX title in a row.

CARGO BIKE
COMPANY: Various
RELEASED: Late 1800s
MATERIAL: Usually steel frame, wooden cargo box
USED FOR: Transporting large loads, especially in cities
Cargo bikes come with either two wheels or three (with two at the front).

CRUISER BIKE
COMPANY: Various
RELEASED: 1930s
MATERIAL: Steel or aluminium
Beach cruisers have one gear, a coaster brake and a relaxed style. They first became popular in the 1930s, and from then until the 1950s they were the most popular bicycle in the United States.

DOWNHILL MOUNTAIN BIKE
COMPANY: GT
RELEASED: 2014 model
MATERIAL: Carbon fibre and alloy
USED FOR: Downhill racing
The bike Rachel Atherton rode to victory in the 2015 Downhill World Championships. With a super-strong frame and wheels, and over 200mm of suspension movement on each wheel, this bike can be ridden down almost anything!

RACE BIKE
COMPANY: AX
RELEASED: August 2015
MATERIAL: Carbon fibre
USED FOR: Road acing
The AX Vial Evo Ultra was the world's lightest racing bike when it was released in 2015. The bike weighs about the same as a chihuahua dog – just 4.4kg!

TOURING BIKE
COMPANY: Koga-Miyata World Traveller
RELEASED: 1999
MATERIAL: Aluminium
USED FOR: Long-distance touring
This bike has actually been used to travel around the world. In fact, in 2008 Mark Beaumont broke the record for the fastest-ever ride around the world. His time for cycling 29,4446km was just 194 days and 17 hours.

Cargo bikes are ideal for moving loads over short distances.

'WORK IT OUT' ANSWERS

for p.4

It takes 12 minutes to walk 1km (60 divided by 5 = 12). It takes 96 minutes (1 hour 36 minutes) to walk 8km (12 x 8 = 96). By bike, you would travel 1km in 5 minutes (60 ÷ 12 = 5). 5 x 8 = 40, so it would take 40 minutes to reach school. This saves 56 minutes: almost an hour.

for p.7

The design brief for the bike for Africa should include:
• Tough • Reliable • Cheap
• Comfortable on bumpy roads
• Easy to repair • Good in dusty and wet/muddy conditions • Able to carry loads
• Suitable for riders of different sizes

for p.11

Design brief:	Alloy?	Steel?
Tough	Less tough	Tougher
Comfortable on bumpy roads	Less comfortable	More comfortable
Reliable	-	-
Cheap	Slightly more expensive	Slightly less expensive
Easy to repair	No	Yes
Good in dry and wet conditions	-	-
Able to carry loads	Yes	Yes
Suitable for riders of different size	-	-

Steel is the best frame material, because it wins nearly every category.

for p.13

Possible ways to add comfort to the hands: shaped grips; a higher handlebar so that less weight is on your hands; a wide, steel handlebar (because steel is flexible, so a wide bar would bend to absorb some of the shock). Ways to add comfort to bottom: a wider, slightly padded saddle; a long, steel seat post.

for p.15

The choices are a curved top tube; a top tube that meets the seat tube further down; or just having a single, big tube connecting the head tube to the rest of the bike. The curved top tube is the strongest choice.

for p.17

Design brief:	26er	29er	27.5er
Tough	3	1	2
Comfortable on bumpy roads	1	3	2
Reliable	3	3	3
Cheap	3	1.5	1.5
Easy to repair	3	1.5	1.5
Good in dry and wet conditions	-	-	-
Able to carry loads	3	1	2
Suitable for riders of different size	3	1	2
Total:	19	12	14

for p.18

The smaller tyre would squash down so much that the tyre might even hit the wheel rim. This often causes a puncture. The bigger tyre will squash down by a similar amount, but not hit the rim.
So the bigger tyre is tougher and more comfortable. It would also be better for carrying heavy loads.

for p.19

In the dry season the road will be dry. In the wet season, most rain falls in the afternoon. So Pamela's ride to school will be dry, and even on her way home it is not likely to be wet and muddy. This means the smooth tyres would probably be best.

for p.21

Design brief:	Derailleur	Hub	Single speed
Tough	1	2	3
Comfortable on bumpy roads	not applicable	-	-
Reliable	1	2	3
Cheap	1.5	1.5	3
Easy to repair	1.5	1.5	3
Good in dry and wet conditions	1	2.5	2.5
Able to carry loads	3	2	1
Suitable for riders of different size	not applicable	-	-
Total:	9	11.5	15.5

for p.22

Pamela's fastest speed would be 294m a minute (70 x 4.2). This is 17640m per hour (294 x 60), which is the same as 17.64kph. Remember, though: no one can pedal at their maximum speed for an hour, or going uphill. Pamela would find it impossible to ride all the way to school at 17.64kph.

for p.24

The main way to carry loads on a bike is using a rack. Racks can be added to the front and/or back of a bike. Bikes designed to carry a passenger or heavy loads almost always use a rear rack.

GLOSSARY

cog circular shape with teeth around the edge

commuter used to travel between home and school/work every day

crank part of a bicycle where the pedal is attached

derailleur moving mechanical arm that changes the gear a bicycle is in

detachable able to be separated or removed

diameter length of a straight line from one side of a circle, through the centre, to the other side

flexible able to bend without breaking

forks part of a bicycle or motorbike that join the front wheel to the frame

gear toothed wheel that controls how fast a rider has to pedal to travel at a particular speed

hub middle part of a wheel rim, the metal outer part of a wheel which the tyre is attached to. Rim brakes press a rubbery pad against the rim to slow down the wheel

locked out made into a non-bouncy fork

rack framework designed for load carrying

reconditioning making something used work as well as it did when it was new

seat post tube connecting a bicycle saddle to the frame

seat tube vertical tube on a bicycle frame, with the seat post and saddle at the top

serviced checked by an expert and given new parts if necessary

slogan short, easily remembered phrase

stand arm or frame that allows a bicycle to stand upright without being held

touring travelling by bicycle carrying everything you need for several days

typeface design of letters; also sometimes called a 'font'

welding using extreme heat to join metal parts together

INDEX